DEAR WEATHER GHOST

DEAR WEATHER GHOST

Melissa Ginsburg

Four Way Books
Tribeca

Please direct all inquiries to:
Editorial Office
Four Way Books
POB 535, Village Station
New York, NY 10014
www.fourwaybooks.com

Library of Congress Cataloging-in-Publication Data

Ginsburg, Melissa.
  Dear weather ghost / Melissa Ginsburg.
    p. cm.
  Poems.
  ISBN 978-1-935536-30-7 (pbk. : alk. paper)
  I. Title.
  PS3607.I4587D43 2013
  811'.6--dc23

2012029328

This book is manufactured in the United States of America
and printed on acid-free paper.

Four Way Books is a not-for-profit literary press. We are grateful for the assistance
we receive from individual donors, public arts agencies, and private foundations.

This publication is made possible with public funds
from the National Endowment for the Arts

and from the New York State Council on the Arts, a state agency.

We are a proud member
of the Council of Literary Magazines and Presses.

Distributed by University Press of New England
One Court Street, Lebanon, NH 03766

Chris

CONTENTS

1.

DRIFT

The birds between poles make a thicker
cable. Their falls dark paper to the broken
soil, blows to cut corn and dirt cuts
a sky. A sky is full stew, a mottle and a glaze.
A road drifts all over our country.

START WITH WHAT YOU KNOW

The rabbit is always in the garden
or in a hole or a mouth
of an animal or a hole in the garden
or a hand: that's how small, a small hole.

Cockroaches fly and get tired.
Prostitutes exist; insects exist.
A hole in the blades which he ate.
A mouth of animals pink in the light.

ARBOR

He was a dancer. He was in the army.
Something happened to him in a small hole,
through his glowing skull. Bones ground together
making a paste. It held us tight as a promise.

Machines were made to hide inside.
Despair a willow of icicles machine
ticking and shrieking from which we could see.
Our trees were. Our machines
arranged to wait for us forever. We chose our trees.
His was a frozen. It covered the horizon. It canopied
a medical leave.

One day he brought me a book he'd been reading.
And I seven times. A pattern on my skin
and the river never. In frozen reverse
the branches attack makes the first
sawdust it makes a nice bed and a nice
smell where did the tree go
where did the sky meet the other sky.

How it happened, none of it was real but it was
winter. He was in the army but he wasn't a dancer.
There was a wall, the bricks needed tuckpointing.
Hollyhocks lived underground covered in rust.
The roots were ready and the rust was ready.
He had to go back to the army and I had to go back to school.
A tree made a floor and the floor stayed.
The world was full of this.

5

PINK BOOK

A factory makes maps and calendars
next to a field containing hay bales.
Inside it seasons. The future
rolls out of a machine.

Sunflower sprouts grow too tall,
rest their leaves in blown soil.
Vines climb the tiger lilies.
Tornadoes rearrange the east.

In a book the typeset is crooked. In Florida
a poem by Elizabeth Bishop. The book
is a pink book. It winters clear.
Saplings, city dies. Baby grows.

NIGHT SHIFT

Between the storage loft and metal stairway
light falls on the rug from a floor above.
A carpet dustglow, clouded hallway.

Night holds hours to the ground
and tucks its trees beneath it.
The trees expect it. Surfaces reflect
the light that's left. Limbs lie dark.

This evening my mother and father
return to their home. My father is tired.
His body performs a bad operation,
in car, flooded street, wrecked garden.

Their house keeps every color inside
but the color of a muck line on a plaster wall.
The sick father holds all colors
but the color of a sick father.

Sometimes the factory makes a kind of shelter.
Machines can be safe here.
The production line can be safe.
Tomorrow I go back to the factory.
I'm getting older like I always wanted.

THE MOSS-THIEF

Clouds rifle through the sunny market.
Flower sellers wait for moss.
Their buds stripe themselves, clamoring
for a secret, for pounds of it.

The sky flips past. Cloud
blows out the damp; a spore could never
settle here. This breeze on an open plain.

In the green shadow of an old stand of forest
the sand was liquid underfoot. Leaf mould
turned into it. I brushed and gathered
the hair of my trees, gray-green

in tumbling bags. It ticked a wide basket
I thought was my heart, beating itself
in the understory.

In the sunny market
the shadow I brought has nothing to cast it.
At market there is nothing to tremble at.
There is nothing in my heart in the sunlight.

One still day in a slurry may I, over the rocks.

LESSONS

I was taught in long rooms,
sun on floor, bored, wanting
a puppy. Learned

the types of hybrids.
Hydrangea rose, mouse
goose, river spider.
On warm tile I used

a spool for a racecar.
I got a puppy once.
It wasn't a good one,

it wouldn't keep.
I learned conversions. Chair
to lock, skirt to curtain,
breath to putrefaction.

Collar converted to trash in
the field. Coyotefish
sputtered in the creek.

ONE DEAD STALK

Catches light. A field, a golden
band, a blue line on the ground.

THE JOB

Not being stupid
I took what was offered: the job
was waiting and I did it

with sand and mirrors, in glitter
while I paced. I waited, I fell
in love with waiting

covered in jewels washed
in from the sea. Summer
kept me in sugared fruits,

shiny shells, mother-of-pearl.
My job was undressing
the sea, what it wanted, shovel

and droplet turned sun to roving dots.
Waiting threw its necklace back,
was work, was softened glass.

BIRTHDAY

I dug a shallow wide hole in the yard
for a tree that might grow or an animal's grave.
Dog in the hole, white fur and fill dirt.
Better to bury it. It was my birthday.

A dogwood in winter has berries the birds like.
A winter rose in the window. A sugar
rose. We will take it in the snow. We'll fill
a hollow log with heated rocks.

It is my birthday. It keeps on, it occurs.
For my birthday I am given a window.
By you I am given. A view, a gift, a tree, a dog,
a stone. Everything I have I give to winter.

MEDICINE

This medicine turns
The sun to poison.
Skin I was. Transparent strips
And blood is nothing. I can use.
Into shop and place of lodging.
Five minutes pass in one direction,
In one lash mark and one
Blindfold wood. The medicine
Turns my food into
A trail the birds eat. Mud
The wasps take. The medicine
Works. Poison I can use.

IN THE COAT CLOSET

I like brown with mink collar. I like gum
in the pockets. Someone will come
when the party is over but the party
chatters on, the guests don't go
to their coaches. I am wearing the pink,
I sleep on the sealskin. Snowdrifts pile, maybe,
keeping them in. Or spring came outside
or everyone died. I hold extra buttons
under my tongue. I keep gloves tight in my hands.

Stone made the mansion as a kind of invitation.
The mansion made the party and the party
the guests. The guests were cold
so they brought coats. The coats grew the closet,
buttons, scarves, friends, gum, bed—
they thickened the dark. I owe the stone.

SEASON

A person walks inside the house
window window other window.
Late fall, leaves pardon themselves
on the lawn. Let the light in,
make the trees responsible.

HOW TO PET A PORCUPINE

My work was important. I hauled icebergs
to the sand. Glass by glass I made my desert
arable. On Mars once watercarved, my robots
collected samples in the vast. My rocks.
My radio, my speakers blown. The sound

stopped. A button popped off. Will never do
what it meant, slip into the hole
rimmed with thread, by machine. Machine
never meant. What I thought. So many stitchings
to do and do and do. Sorting through old clothes.

Sweaters. Shoes. What I mean is
Does the sand care, does it want
an heir. The sand once childrened
my wants, kept layers, planets, I built myself
a farm. But the rock was marred. The relapse

was happening. At a certain point
you can stop it and at a certain point
you can't. The dining room sanded my table
of ungratefuls. My distinguished. Once adorabled.
Now charmed smiles, soup in the mouth. Elegant,

coiffed and firelit. I inhabit and wait and inhabit
and wait while food and emptiness
trade places. Sand scars my eyes, red sketches
the whites, a penny blossoms
green at the bottom of my glass. Surface

tension holds the bugs up, holds water over the rim.
Gravity lays me low. My water, my gravity. Devoted
and grateful to the applied sciences, I am watching
rocks get cleaned in a machine. In science class
I measured, what was the punch line? Very carefully.

IN THE YARD

I heard a kitten behind the fence
crying so terribly it became a machine.
Once it was a machine I couldn't help it.

2.

SQUAB

I was in love in the library. I had a perch, and a future
life in symbols. I'd been listening to the radio.

The kitchen bubbled a bath of wilting leaves, a sauce
thick with blood and a half-spoon of vinegar.

In the hall of books the swinging perch and doll eyes wobbled.
A song came on. A dove song.

Empty of bones full of liver without gall my heart
open, the blood clot which forms in the middle removed.

Arrange my heart on a round plate. It is a small heart
and a small plate, the doll's a girl at the window plays with.

Stop, warm library. Stop square window, tender symbol. Stop
little girl the peacemaker, wooden grip and polished nickel.

She was going to miss me, miss all of us.
She was hungry, listening to the song.

APRIL

By the phlox and lilac weather
was not. The sky was white. Sun went
in the street. Wind waved

pelts to petals. Moved bits
of garden around. One piece touched
a different piece. Wind put the pieces back.

The sun got in the car. A garden
touched a garden, more or less.
The milkweed touched a fence.

THE MAPLE TREE

The stupid wind a memory
of the long and delicate animal I once cared for

near the maple tree. Behind it though it did not hide us.
Somehow I had skipped a season, confused

by the maple leaves' tenacity, dead purple
moving to gray and hanging on.

Winter turned my pet to fur, tore the air
around me into cold. The creature

betrayed me in spring. He killed half the villagers
I hoped to one day meet

and become friends with
in their brightly colored coats and scarves.

For months they cut snowflakes out of paper
and taped them to the windows.

It seemed like an attractive lifestyle.
I hadn't lived through anything much.

TURDUCKEN

Heavy above the scratch in the barnyard
hens cluck. Chicks in their limited eggs rock side to side.

Storm captivates sky. The house
at the top of the hill is the color of shadow.

Rain marries the ground, Holsteins lose their contrast.
The hill flattens, swallows bales of hay, stuffs itself

with a layer of pond, with outbuildings. A lightning
throws the oak in flames, warms its chipmunks living inside.

The fire gives some shadows back, but shakes them.
We once had a cavity, too, and were inflamed

by it, so took out our bones and laid ourselves open
in new acquaintanceship: exterior not.

Interior not. Density yes. We are one animal,
our mistakes are hidden, tucked in the bigger bird of us.

We would accomplish much without bones.
Didn't the kitchen have plenty of light, and room?

MERMAID

Flood deeps the shallows.
The rivers get covered.

We difficult our dinners.
In times of hunger, if only

a rock on which to perch.
In sleep we choose a dream:

lure a gull and water lock it,
meet a boy and get feet.

MORNING

Waves suck at the fallen pines and rocks
at the base of the bluff.

Tide abandons. The morning
leaks. Sun, no clouds, the usual breezes,

dogs in the water. Boughs,
endless needles. On the old pilings

the pelicans wait, holding
their wings out to dry.

Sand buries the bones of wading birds,
long and light.

DEAR DECAY

On Thursday I nailed a sign in the yard.
I've spent most of my life helping birds. The rest
I've just wasted. You saw it, everyone saw it
carry the disease. An air full of birds, wild
magpie, pheasant, owl. A doorway full.
Decay, I won't refuse the crying tern.
His visit claws the living room.

Last night through a window you entered
as I slept. My dear silent partner.
Past the curtains. Near the stove. The long
bent stick with a foot on it lay alone
by the open door. Decay, Dear broken-winged,
you are moving at a rate. Coos. Wild
particles. Swiftly down the hall.

HERON

I was great and blue and standing still,
alone until the summer—long away,
through cold and over ponds—
water pushing small dawns
apart in quartz-bright waves, in swash
and undertow. My knees were fixed
forever straight. Summer flew
false through the sky.

In shallow pools in winter, needles
floating can be read from high enough
above their slack they make a kind of map.
The needle trees flash messages. Tides
flatten minnows. Rocks they smooth
and loosen. We flapped our wings,
never left the marsh's muck. The map
and us is for the sky, that surface
laid above itself, pine-struck.

A BOWLING BALL

fell through the river to the river's bed
where everything ends up rounded eventually

if not on this afternoon, this accident: the cataract
of time. The weeping scene will grow into scenery,

the waterweight gratefully above. Elsewhere
what it carries landing and spinning.

Its dead buoyancy, all its holes filled.
Its finger-lungs resting, its gathered pressure.

It stays like that. Ducks float over, three shadows
lapping light from the surface, the sun.

VATEL

On a Friday
    seamy   with expense
              the king's men

    laid a table.   Fine volatiles for a thousand guests.

Oceans of the world
    held tide   to chest

      asift   with starfish.

Appetite
palaced   the corners of the kitchen

        yet away from the coast

  all delicacies swam.

        One cart of mussels

        would not satisfy   would not
                 survive the night.

Chef Vatel

forsook the empty kettles

        for his quarters.

The dinner served
           hunger served
           failure.

    Vatel's sword
        happened to his heart.

        Weaving hung   to keep the cold out
                    did not keep the cold out.

Gold filigreed the nightstand.

SPRING

A row of trimmed hedge
without leaves has caught
and held a line of leaves shed
from above all winter.
A flitting brightness takes the form
of a cardinal in morning sun. Jonquils
furl in their bulbs. Trapped buds
time their chance.

THE DISSECTION

Each girl gets a pretty frogtray
and a dead pet and a ribbon
to dress it. Each pet gets a drink
of long life and sacrifice
and lemonade and lemons, lies down
in the black putty in a tin bed and wears
the wedding pins.

Willingly. A girl wears the pins
on her lapel, laced with instinct,
a bad story, long and messy
favorite subject. Each pet
and each girl wears the pins
and learns lessons, sketched anatomy,
a love, a place to rest.

Each pet lies patient
for the busride home.

3.

Dear Weather Ghost,

You work a lazy promise and a mess
of beds blown over. A wallpaper eraser
and a smoother. You beat a rock and show
its insides, frozen as a predator
spotting a target.

I keep a rock like that one
in my pocket. I am waiting for you
to come and clean it. I'll take charity
from killers if I need it.

Dear Weather Ghost,

On the beach I watched
the bluff erode. Veneer
inside me. Come on,
I'm a pretty audience.

Trash trees splintered,
stabbed. I stood inside
the eye but eye of what.
Who did the world go

back inside. The hurricane
ant shears a leaf. See, veneer
covers a vacuum and the problem
sleeps. The woods are weak.

Dear Weather Ghost,

I left home for you. I came far.

I poured escape
on your downturned
glass. I shattered a pitcher.

I was suspicion. I was
elsewhere. I nailed
the competition.

My night closed the window.

Curtains drawn, I was
attempting a feeling.

Dear Weather Ghost,

Heat stays in the oven and won't come out.

Your clouds gather;

                        they flock and school
and kill.

          I'm cold,

drawing charts to gravity,

                      feeding the oven

cornfields and funnel clouds.

          From my lungs take my captive

             air. Take gravity,

      its birthdays   clicking their needles.

Make me forget,

          marry me,
              make the cyclones touch.

Dear Weather Ghost,

Your sunset careless with stars
showing. Say stars show time
people pray to: Let me try
to take care of you and fail. Let me
be asleep when you come home.

Dear Weather Ghost,

When I held dead July in my arms
you would not even let me do that.

Don't visit.

Dear Weather Ghost,

For once I was
the architect

setting fire at the fencepost
to dry needles.

When the flame delivers me
it looks at you. It is laughable.

I like such length and view.

The flame exits your tasteless
operation, and so on:

I will crash,
have not qualified.

Dear Weather Ghost,

A dune of the outside builds in me.
I am not exiled, I am remote lands.
I'll order my acre.

4.

PRESERVE

Silkflower and snowevil brittle
by the roadside. By salt-stained.
In a cloudy dark. In roads. In a field
to the north close to the known
precarious border in the field.
Was the border. It faces north. Lace
and thorn. You can't pick
those flowers, they shatter! Across
the border clouds are different.
Snowevil denser, petals more
translucent. They burn something
in their factory. All summer they die.
All permanent winter.

IN THE KITCHEN

Stove rests on a fir floor, a soft wood
black at the nails. Fruits press the jar walls.
The ceiling fan slices a circle near the ceiling.
A safety pin pulls the palm's skin, the bored
mutilation of a child. The kitchen overlaps
another kitchen where the plates are fired
bonedust in the cabinet and light bulbs work
for a thousand hours. The refrigerator fills
with weight and room. It will keep on
making that sound.

BIRTHDAY

Sam says: *a man steals something and runs*
toward home. He sees a man in a mask
so he runs back. You have to guess the situation.
I guess diseases, airborne

as insects. It's my birthday. A bee lands.
Coneflowers sag into the yard.
Sam says he has put the answer in my mind
with his mind and it's up to me to see it.

I've heard this riddle before, but I guess
for an hour and never think *baseball*.
My guesses are star shaped,
infestations boring.

It's September. Coneflower season is over.
The sun blinds and does not stop.

IN THE COURTYARD

I live near the dried up fountain. The master is gone.
The servants are gone. I was one of them;
I was the one who put the kettle on.
Mornings I called for the house to wake.
One day it would not wake
in a growl and hiss, pushing its hard parts against me.
It seems clear a mistake was made; perhaps it was I
who made the mistake.

Teatime, birds come. The scones pile up.
I guess I bake them for the birds. Pick and flutter.
Master's orders circle, knock against each other
like tall grasses, an animal rustling through them,
an animal nowhere in the field. I was never
an animal on the makeshift prairie but I did
what I could. Said yes to everything.
Swept stones into the corners.

BIRTHDAY

Story in a lily pond a very tiny girl.
Rough crystal, pistil and stamen,

stem a clear stream. Flowers are
a house. Flowers cover the birthday cake.

The cake came to a party.
Came past the garbage,

sugared. On a petal she ate.
Fish cut

the stem in two, for travel.
The waterways opened and a bird helped her

for whom she was grateful and developed affection.
Pulsed calls. Rare whistled songs

under the water.
As for the party

How far I was. Now in a flower I'm on fire
said the cake.

Memory. I'm done with memory
said the blossom.

Do not feed the flowers. Please
said a sign.

BOWL

The future lay fallow in the palm of my hand.
My hand kept closing, menacing.
A blank space in the season,
a draft through the kitchen, quarter moons
cutting my palm. Electricity, leafburn,
the food squirrels bury.
Pale arm lifting to a high thing on a shelf.
A bowl, a jar. There was nothing
there. Blue enamel on it, cold to touch.

OUR HOSPITAL

We made a hospital in our house. We made a crutch
and a folding bed. We made a tray of instruments.
We made green walls and a sunny window and a poster
of a flower. The taps ran rust. It convinced us.
We made a few patients and taught them how to act,
to stumble and bleed, in turn, here and there.

Our hospital filled. The patients grew thin.
We drew pictures of their minds and colored them in.
Some of them didn't "make it."
We emptied the pictures and took down the poster. Finally,
our hospital loved us.

When your hospital loves you it lives inside you.
Its walls are green and its carpet is blue. It has white
and grey fibers, light blue and dark blue, seams
and stains. The carpet is filled with not having "made it."
There are shadows, boring shadows. Shadows of a table
all over it.

WAVE

Air ate the inside of my lungs repeatedly.
Air shoved the seabed.
Ocean stepped back, its mansions gasping.

The new shore.
I came down to look.
Passed elephants stampeding to safety.

Seabed lavished me.
Waves made rooms.
Salt crystals built me walls and dissolved.

Elephants shivered on an olivine crag,
still in certain ways alive, though
from the dead come precious carvings.

MY DAUGHTER

I burned with hot oil
a girl I was

baking. I was no
pretty one.

I made the children

go outside and take
their bangs and plaits.

*

Summer was green
and closed

as the past, as
accidents.

There were many.

*

Well you were a young.
The cake was lopsided

and I wanted danger
in the form of deep feeling:

adulthood of accidents, many
and scattered.

*

Fan blew a sugar
storm over the kitchen.

I wanted it
and I had it.

THE GAME

We played shooting each other
in the slow gray afternoon yard.
I shot you twice on the heart.
We walked to the farmhouse
hospital, the surgery bedroom.

In there, in some prairied life
we'd made love all afternoon
and staggered to the golden dusk,
a walnut tree in the distance.

Now the chill held gold to hide behind,
thinly. It was to be
the last such day and everybody knew it.

For a week I waited. On the porch
on painted boards.
While you slept we traded hearts
and married again in the folding bed.

In your hand the harvest:
your chest, my gun.
I was going to tell you.
Tissues knitted in the cold.

ANNIVERSARY POEM

Warehouse, factory. Picnic table,
planted maple. Swallows sunlight
the continent. Beyond a bright morning
a forest endangered. In a row,
yellow, building. Distant sunlight,
hungry swallows caves. In the,
even in, shadowy. I, mosses, you.

THE SEA

In the solace of my dog's mouth
I left a screaming rabbit.
Her mouth shines black as sea.

THE RABBIT

Once I was a milliner's apprentice.
I served a master. I tried hard

among his charts.
He toiled, fringed poppies.

I loved our caged rabbit in the dim room.
Pink half of a pair bond.

I wove and steamed. I wooled and tweeded.
Yards of felt I ruined.

In the dim room I caged and charted.
I poppied a pillbox. I lumped a cloche.

I bowed. I halved and pinked and pinned.
I failed lappets. Pinners and paste.

I laced and edged and ribboned.
A hat apprenticed the rabbit.

Rabbit served and dimmed.
My failure owed the milliner a favor.

It fell upon a button and a feather.
It caged the cap and set the rabbit master.

SEASON

On storm cleaned land
soy sprouted in dark rows.
A green field spread to the edge
with cows on it.

That was the world, us two
in rooms and outside.
Looking through the window.
Jerking a hand away. A dog
barked. That was spring.

IN THE TREEHOUSE

I broke these twigs for you and put them on a plate.
Your tea will keep.

ACKNOWLEDGMENTS

Caketrain; Capgun; Copper Nickel; C R O W D; DIAGRAM; Forklift, Ohio; Gulf Coast; Konundrum Engine Literary Review; Pleiades; Seneca Review; The Iowa Review

Several of the poems in this book originally appeared in the chapbook *Arbor* (New Michigan Press, 2007).

Melissa Ginsburg grew up in Houston, Texas, and is the author of *Arbor*, a chapbook published by New Michigan Press. Her poems have appeared in *Forklift, Ohio*; *The Iowa Review*; *jubilat*; *Pleiades*; and other magazines. She holds an MFA from the Iowa Writers' Workshop and lives in Oxford, Mississippi, where she teaches creative writing at the University of Mississippi and edits the literary magazine *Yalobusha Review*.